Global Business Trends

英語でみる世界の大学生の就職事情

Iwao Yamashita
Atsuko Nishimura
Derek Eberl
Masamichi Asama

Global business Trends

Copyright © 2015

by

Iwao Yamashita

Atsuko Nishimura

Derek Eberl

Masamichi Asama

All Rights Reserved
No part of this book may be reproduced in any form without written permission from the authors and Nan'un-do Co., Ltd.

このテキストのCD音声を無料で視聴（ストリーミング）・ダウンロードできます。自習用音声としてご活用ください。
以下のサイトにアクセスしてテキスト番号で検索してください。

https://nanun-do.com　テキスト番号 [511693]

※ 無線LAN（WiFi）に接続してのご利用を推奨いたします。
※ 音声ダウンロードはZipファイルでの提供になります。
　お使いの機器によっては別途ソフトウェア（アプリケーション）の導入が必要となります。

Global Business Trends 音声ダウンロードページは左記のQRコードからもご利用になれます。

21世紀に入り、日本の社会や産業界が急速にグローバル化しつつある中、大学教育もグローバル化に積極的に取り組み、構造転換を果たすことが求められています。特に英語教育には、その先兵として大きな期待が集まっているところであります。本テキストはそういった大学教育のあり方や背景を視野に入れ、幅広く世界15か国の大学生の多様な就職状況をメイントピックとし、世界各国の同年代の若者の仕事に対する考え方や就職方法を文化的背景と共に紹介し、学習者にとって新たな知的発見の契機になるよう編まれたものです。各ユニットの構成は以下のようになっております。

Listening Practice

　その国を代表する企業の紹介する英文を聞いて、簡単な問題に答えながら当該国への関心や意識の高揚を図ることになります。

Vocabulary, Grammar & Reading Comprehension

　日本人学生と当該国の学生との会話文を読みながら、並べ替えや空所補充の問題に答えることになります。ここでは、当該国の就職状況は言うまでもなく、それ以外にもその国の学生の仕事に対する考え方や英語学習の状況、いま人気のある職種などバラエティに富んだトピックによるダイアログが展開され、学習者はさらに当該国への関心を深めることが期待されます。

TOEIC Reading Practice & Vocabulary

　当該国の英語（語学）学習状況を紹介する英文を読むことにより、自身が置かれた状況と比較しつつ、英語学習に対する意識を先鋭化してゆきます。

　本テキストによる英語学習が、単なる英語習得に終始するだけでなく、これから国際人として巣立ってゆくために必要不可欠な知識と教養の基礎を身につける一助となれば幸いです。
　最後に、本テキスト出版に際して、南雲堂編集部の加藤敦さんに企画立案の段階から編集に至るまで様々なアドバイスをいただき、大変お世話になりました。この場を借りて心より御礼申し上げます。

著者一同

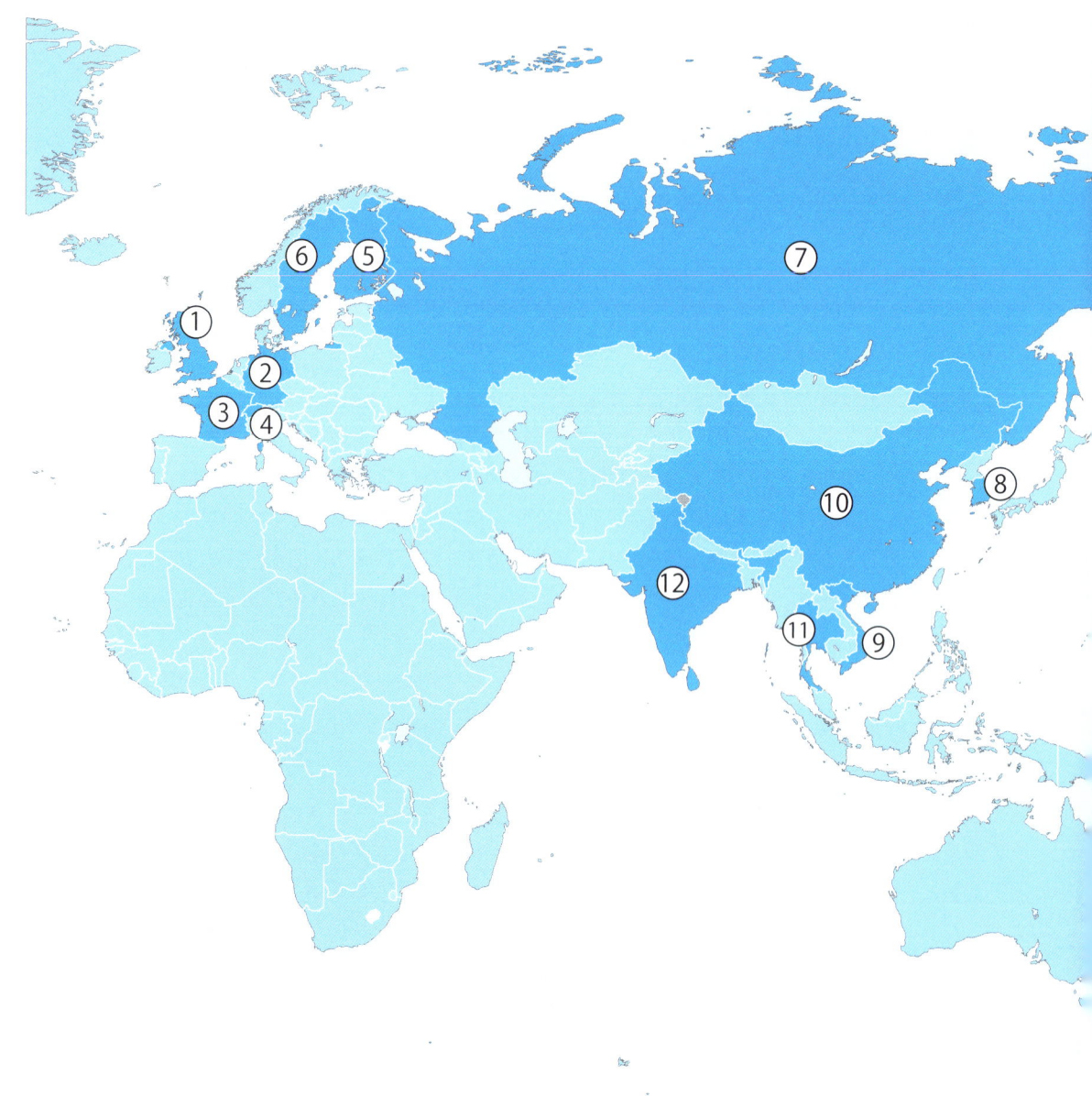

Contents

Unit 1	The United Kingdom	Virgin Atlantic	6
Unit 2	Germany	Adidas	10
Unit 3	France	Louis Vuitton	14
Unit 4	Switzerland	Nestlé	18
Unit 5	Finland	Rovio	22
Unit 6	Sweden	IKEA	26
Unit 7	Russia	Gazprom	30

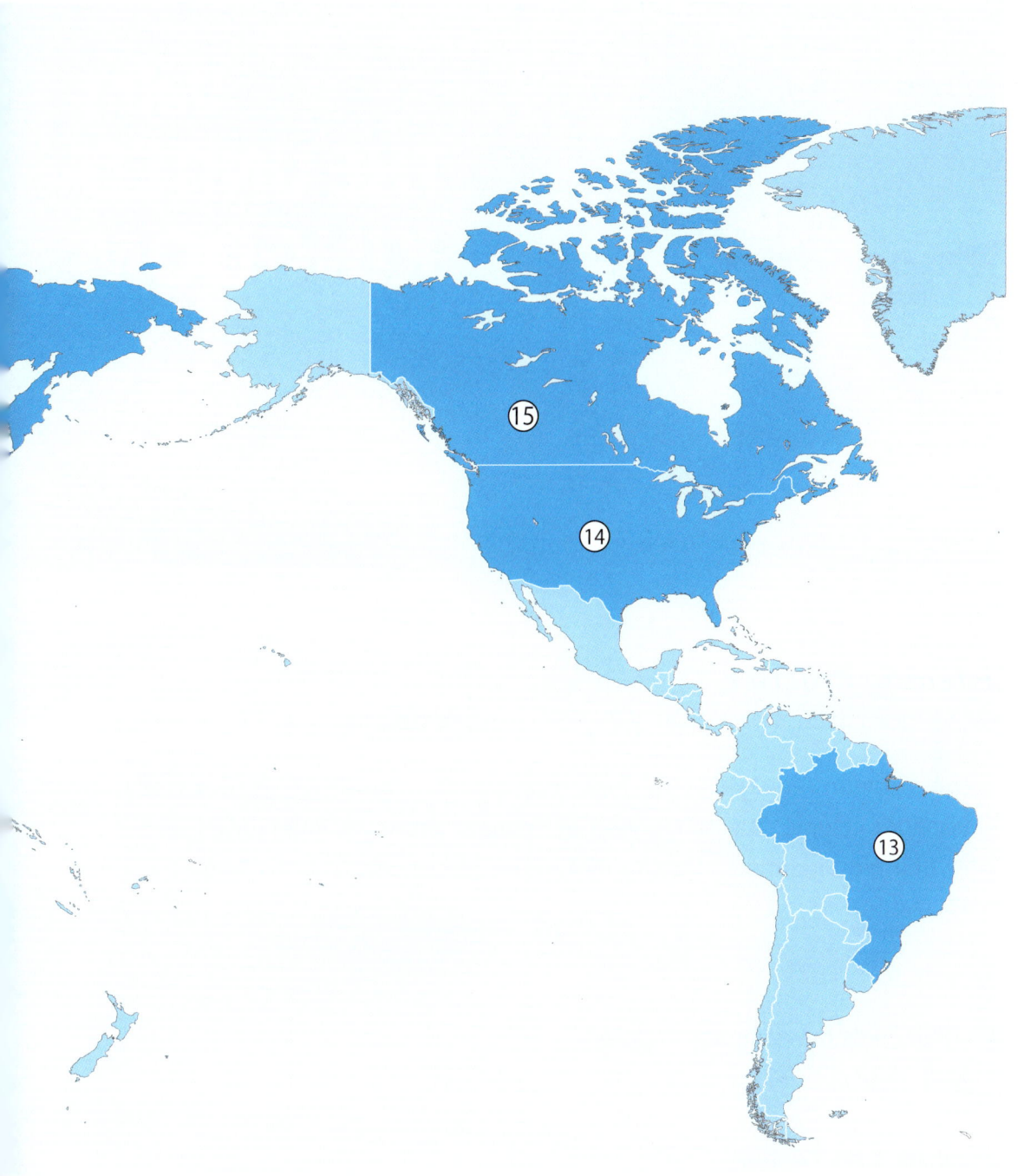

Unit 8	South Korea	Samsung	34
Unit 9	Vietnam	Vinamilk	38
Unit 10	China	China Mobile Limited	42
Unit 11	Thailand	Siam Cement Group	46
Unit 12	India	Tata Motors	50
Unit 13	Brazil	Bug Agentes Biológicos	54
Unit 14	The United States of America	Coca Cola	58
Unit 15	Canada	Louis Garneau	62

Unit 1
THE UNITED KINGDOM

イギリスでは、航空業や運輸、携帯、音楽業界に新たな旋風を巻き起こしたヴァージングループが注目されています。

Listening Practice 2

次の出だし英文を読んでから、そのあとに流れる英文を聴き、1.〜3.の問いに適当な答えを (A)〜(C) より選びなさい。

Virgin Atlantic Airways is the eighth-largest British airline in terms of passenger volume. It was founded by Richard Branson, and started with only one old airplane, a Boeing B747-200, at London Gatwick Airport in 1984.

1. What made the company popular?
   (A)   (B)   (C)

2. Where does it operate?
   (A)   (B)   (C)

3. Who is Richard Branson?
   (A)   (B)   (C)

6

Vocabulary, Grammar & Reading Comprehension

次の会話文を読んで下の問いに答えなさい。

イギリス留学に憧れる Atsuko は、イギリスの大学生の間で人気のギャップイヤーについて英会話の先生 Chris に尋ねます。

Atsuko: Do you A[a / year / is / know / gap / what]?

Chris: Yes. A gap year is a sabbatical, or time off. It (A) a period of time, not necessarily a year, in which students take a break from school and may travel or use this time to undertake activities they enjoy.

Atsuko: I see… In Japan, Tokyo University announced that they would (B) taking a gap year. How about in your country? Is taking a gap year common in the U.K.?

Chris: Yes. I guess about 10% of university students take a gap year. Universities B[a year / to / students / take / allow] off before they enter university.

Atsuko: What do students usually do during their gap year?

Chris: Some work or (C) volunteer activities, and others travel or go abroad for a working holiday. During their gap year they can have outside-the-box experiences by (D) different people, cultures, languages, and social models. They have experiences which are different from those of their everyday lives.

Atsuko: That sounds exciting! In Japan, the concept of a gap year is not well known. That's most likely due to the typical Japanese (E) system. Job-hunting starts when university students are juniors.

---

sabbatical 研究目的のため大学教員などに与えられる有給休暇、元来は 7 年ごとに 1 年間与えられる
outside-the-box 型にはまらない　junior 大学 3 年生

問 1. 文中の（ A ）から（ E ）に入れるのに最も適当なものを下からそれぞれ選びなさい。

　　engage in　　employment　　refers to　　encountering　　promote

問 2. 文中の A、B の [ ] 内の語を正しい順番に並べ替えて意味が通るようにしなさい。

A _____
B _____

問 3. 下の 1.〜 3. の英文が会話の内容に合っていれば T、間違っていれば F を選びなさい。

1. T F In Britain, one out of ten students take a year off before they begin university.
2. T F Many universities in Japan encourage students to take a gap year.
3. T F Most Japanese students begin searching for a job during their last year at university.

TOEIC Reading Practice & Vocabulary

次の英文を読んで下の問に答えなさい。

The financial industry of the U.K. has a long history. Life insurance, for example, originated in England in the 17th century. A career in finance is still of great interest to British university students searching for jobs, even after the financial crisis faced by major banks, such as the Royal Bank of Scotland (RBS). If you're seeking a job in finance in the U.K., your best course of action would be to become a chartered certified accountant. This means you must obtain the Association of Chartered Certified Accountants (ACCA) Qualification, and become a member of the ACCA. Founded in 1904, the ACCA is the global body for professional accountants (The "charter" referred to in the name, is the Royal Charter granted to the association by the sovereign in 1974). An ACCA Qualification provides you with skills and knowledge relevant to any type of business. That means you're free to choose the accountancy role and organization you want to work for. It shows that you have completed studies in relevant areas, have 36 months' experience in a relevant role, and have completed the Professional Ethics module.

Royal Bank of Scotland 王立スコットランド銀行（1727 年設立）　**chartered** 公認された = certified　**global body** 国際的組織　**Royal Charter**（英国の国王）に承諾された特許状　**sovereign** 主権者、国家元首　**Professional Ethics module** 職業倫理のコース

Unit 1

問 1. 本文の内容に合うように、(A)～(D) の中から最も適当なものを選びなさい。

1. The U.K. financial industry -------.
    (A) doesn't include life insurance
    (B) originated in the 17th century
    (C) is popular among job seekers in the U.K.
    (D) has never experienced financial crisis

2. If you're interested in a career in the financial industry, -------.
    (A) RBS, a major bank, is recommended
    (B) the Royal Charter will be very supportive
    (C) the ACCA will help you with job hunting
    (D) you should obtain an official ACCA qualification

3. ACCA -------.
    (A) was established at the beginning of the 20th century
    (B) is a national organization of higher education
    (C) grants a charter to you by the sovereign
    (D) has been one of the most successful banks

4. The ACCA Qualification -------.
    (A) is the global body for professional accountants
    (B) is proof of your experience and skills as an accountant
    (C) enables you to be the best accountant in any organization
    (D) can be acquired without an exam or professional experience

問 2. 次の定義が意味する語（句）を本文中から選びなさい。
1. a time of great danger   (   )
2. the activity of managing money   (   )
3. a person whose job is to keep or check financial accounts   (   )
4. closely connected with the subject you are discussing   (   )
5. to pass an examination, or officially complete a course   (   )

9

Unit 2
GERMANY

ドイツはスポーツ大国です。ここでは皆さんもよく知っている Adidas 社をとりあげます。

Listening Practice 4

次の出だし英文を読んでから、そのあとに流れる英文を聴き、1.〜3.の問いに適当な答えを (A)〜(C) より選びなさい。

Adolf 'Adi' Dassler started making his own sports shoes in his mother's laundry house after returning home from World War I.

1. When did Adi's brother, Rudi, begin helping him make shoes?
   (A)   (B)   (C)

2. Why did the Dassler brothers create two separate companies?
   (A)   (B)   (C)

3. What did Rudy name his company?
   (A)   (B)   (C)

Vocabulary, Grammar & Reading Comprehension

次の会話文を読んで下の問いに答えなさい。

> 日本の大学でドイツ語を学ぶ Mari は、将来ドイツの会社に就職したいと考えています。先日、学内で知り合ったドイツからの留学生 Dieter にドイツの就職事情について尋ねています。

Mari: Will it be difficult for you to find a job in Germany after you graduate from university?

Dieter: No, not really. There is always a strong (A) for computer and electrical engineers in the German automobile industry.

Mari: Is that right? What company are you (B)?

Dieter: I'm planning to work for Volkswagen. ᴬ[last year / of / my friends / a few / graduated / who] are working there now, and are saying good things about it. They've learned a lot, and there's plenty of (C) for advancement.

Mari: Really? That sounds great! Volkswagen is one of the top automakers in the world. What a wonderful opportunity!

Dieter: Yeah, they are the largest automobile (D) in Europe, and the third largest in the world. They have factories in many different countries.

Mari: You'll probably have to travel a lot. You'll get to see many (E) places.

Dieter: I hope so. ᴮ[they / don't / have / I / think / a factory] in Japan, but I know they have one in China. If I travel there in the future, I'll be sure to visit you in Japan.

問 1. 文中の（A）から（E）に入れるのに最も適当なものを下からそれぞれ選びなさい。

> opportunity   demand   manufacturer   different   targeting

問 2. 文中の A、B の [ ] 内の語を正しい順番に並べ替えて意味が通るようにしなさい。

A _____
B _____

問 3. 下の 1.～3. の英文が会話の内容に合っていれば T、間違っていれば F を選びなさい。

1. T F   The automobile industry in Germany today needs engineers.
2. T F   There are some Volkswagen factories located outside of Europe, too.
3. T F   Dieter would like to visit the Volkswagen factories in Japan and China.

TOEIC Reading Practice & Vocabulary

次の英文を読んで下の問に答えなさい。

Though the German education system differs in many ways from that of other countries, it produces well-educated and high-performing students.

Children from the age of three to six usually attend kindergarten, although it's not required. After that, however, education is compulsory for the next nine to ten years. From grades one through four, children attend elementary school (Grundschule). Here the education is the same for all students and everyone studies the basic subjects. After the fourth grade, however, students are divided up according to academic ability, according to the wishes of their parents. Afterwards, they attend either Hauptschule, Realschule or Gymnasium. Students who want to enter university must attend Gymnasium.

Gymnasium is a selective school that offers promising students a quality liberal arts education. It prepares students for university, and leads to a prestigious diploma called the Abitur. Students can receive this diploma only after passing all examinations. The Abitur also contains all of the student's grades, and formally enables him or her to attend university. Thus, the Abitur functions not only as a graduation certificate, but as an academic transcript and university entrance exams. This important document also gives much prestige and social status to the students who worked so hard to receive it.

---

compulsory 義務制の　**Hauptschule** 基幹学校（義務教育の延長として小学校高学年から中学校に相当する5年制の職業教育を施す）　**Realschule** 実務学校（Hauptschuleと同じく職業教育を施すが、期間は6年で実務訓練だけでなく高等教育準備もできる）　**Gymnasium** 大学への進学を希望する生徒たちが進学する8年制の学校。日本の中高一貫校に近い。　**promising** 前途有望な　**liberal arts** 一般教養　**diploma** 資格証明書

Unit 2

問 1. 本文の内容に合うように、(A)〜(D) の中から最も適当なものを選びなさい。

1. The German education system requires -------.
   (A) all children from the ages of nine and ten to go to elementary school
   (B) children to attend school from the age of seven until they are about 16 or 17
   (C) parents to decide what secondary school their children should attend
   (D) students to take an entrance examination to enter Gymnasium

2. German students -------.
   (A) all study the same subjects while in primary school
   (B) decide if they should attend university in the future
   (C) must attend three different types of schools to graduate
   (D) must pass the entrance examination for Gymnasium

3. The German Gymnasium is -------.
   (A) a large building where students can play sports
   (B) required for all students who study hard and do well
   (C) a special school for students who want to attend university
   (D) one of the most respected universities in all of Germany

4. The Abitur is an important document that -------.
   (A) allows a student to pass an entrance examination
   (B) a student needs to enter a university in Germany
   (C) students can use to get into liberal arts classes
   (D) German companies use to hire new employees

問 2. 次の定義が意味する語（句）を本文中から選びなさい。

1. a place where education is introduced to young children　（　　　　　）
2. respect gained by someone because of their success in society　（　　　　　）
3. a document that proves graduation　（　　　　　）
4. an education program that provides a broad general education　（　　　　　）
5. a document proving that you have completed a course of study or passed an exam　（　　　　　）

Unit 3
FRANCE

Louis Vuitton は、Moët Hennessy という会社を併合し、今や LVMH と呼ばれる企業にまで成長しています。

Listening Practice 6

次の出だし英文を読んでから、そのあとに流れる英文を聴き、1.～3.の問いに適当な答えを (A)～(C) より選びなさい。

Louis Vuitton has long been one of the most popular French brand names in the global fashion industry, and is known for its strong marketing campaigns. Due to the company's effective marketing strategy, today they're a well-known prestige brand.

1. What happened in 1987?
   (A)   (B)   (C)

2. What is true of Moët Hennessy?
   (A)   (B)   (C)

3. What do French students think about LVMH?
   (A)   (B)   (C)

strategy 方策　prestige 権威、名門

Vocabulary, Grammar & Reading Comprehension

次の会話文を読んで下の問いに答えなさい。

日本の大学でフランス語を学ぶKeisukeは、フランス人の英語力に関する調査を行っています。そこで、フランスからの留学生Laurentに質問しています。

Keisuke: Our English teacher said that when he visited Paris about 30 years ago, French people didn't even try to speak English, though they understood what he was saying when he spoke to them in English. He was surprised that their English was so poor.

Laurent: I'm not surprised about your teacher's experience. Now the level of spoken English in France is slowly improving. Many people say France (A) has the weakest English skills in Europe, though most European countries successfully (B) high English proficiency.

Keisuke: It is very hard to imagine, but ᴬ**[do you think / French people's English proficiency / how poor / is]**? Do you have any (C)?

Laurent: Yes. According to a certain international education company, France ranked 35 out of 60 countries where English is the second language. It is ranked last among all European countries, and is also behind China, Taiwan; and is just ahead of the United Arab Emirates.

Keisuke: I read somewhere that the reason for poor English proficiency is partly because French people are protective of their own language. Do they have ᴮ**[their own / of / a fear / unique culture and language / losing]**?

Laurent: That is the wrong (D). Sweden serves as a good example. They are ranked number one in the world for English as a second language proficiency, and, (E), they have maintained their own language and culture.

United Arab Emirates アラブ首長国連邦

問1. 文中の（ A ）から（ E ）に入れるのに最も適当なものを下からそれぞれ選びなさい。

statistics　　at the same time　　currently　　mentality　　demonstrate

問2. 文中のA、Bの[ ]内の語を正しい順番に並べ替えて意味が通るようにしなさい。

A _____
B _____

問 3. 下の 1. 〜 3. の英文が会話の内容に合っていれば T、間違っていれば F を選びなさい。

1. T F Keisuke's English teacher enjoyed speaking with French people in English when he visited Paris 30 years ago.
2. T F Chinese people have higher English proficiency than French people.
3. T F Swedish people's English proficiency is very high because they're not concerned about protecting their own language.

TOEIC Reading Practice & Vocabulary

次の英文を読んで下の問に答えなさい。

PSA Peugeot Citroën, a major French manufacturer of automobiles and motorcycles selected World Speaking, a globally-recognized company which specializes in distance learning tools, to train their global staff so English will be the common language used by company employees. In April of 2010, a joint decision was made by PSA and World Speaking, to train 10,000 employees in 25 countries, with the aim of achieving an "operational" level of English throughout the organization over a three-year period. World Speaking has agreed to give free lessons to anyone that has not reached an acceptable level of English within that time-frame. A wide range of training courses are offered, including individual telephone lessons, group workshops via video-conferencing, virtual classrooms, and an online preparation course for TOEIC, the Test of English for International Communication.

A PSA spokesperson said: "This course is for anyone who needs to work internationally. This includes people who are selling cars, as well as those who needs to communicate with colleagues in our international subsidiaries. In less than a year, 3,800 employees enrolled in the program, and offered positive feedback about it."

distance learning 遠隔学習（インターネット等を利用して遠隔地から教育を受ける学習形態）
time-frame 時間枠　**video-conference** テレビ会議　**subsidiary** 子会社

Unit 3

問 1. 本文の内容に合うように、(A)〜(D) の中から最も適当なものを選びなさい。

1. Peugeot started an English language training program for employees because the company -------.
   (A) plans to have a branch office in London
   (B) plans to employ a lot of British students
   (C) is going to use English as the common language inside the company
   (D) wants to sell more cars in the U.K.

2. World Speaking -------.
   (A) is in charge of PSA Peugeot English language training
   (B) specializes in developing English learning tools
   (C) is an organization which promotes the TOEIC test
   (D) has 10,000 language trainers worldwide

3. People taking English lessons will NOT receive -------.
   (A) telephone lessons
   (B) lessons in a virtual classroom
   (C) a certificate for international business English qualification
   (D) group lessons

4. According to a PSA spokesperson, -------.
   (A) this language program is only for employees who want to sell more cars
   (B) the employees taking this course are satisfied with this program
   (C) this program is mainly targeted to those who want to improve their TOEIC scores
   (D) employees taking this program should be very motivated

問 2. 次の定義が意味する語（句）を本文中から選びなさい。

1. ready for use, or able to be used ( )
2. a company that is owned or controlled by a holding company ( )
3. someone whom you work with ( )
4. by means of, by using ( )
5. to officially join a course ( )

17

Unit 4
SWITZERLAND

スイスには国際機関や多国籍企業の本社がたくさんあります。ここでは食品会社ネスレを紹介します。

Listening Practice 8

次の出だし英文を読んでから、そのあとに流れる英文を聴き、1.～3.の問いに適当な答えを (A)～(C) より選びなさい。

Nestlé was founded in 1866 in Switzerland, where their headquarters are still located today. It provides consumers all over the world with a wide range of foods and beverages.

1. How many workers does Nestlé have?
   (A)　(B)　(C)

2. How can you apply for a job?
   (A)　(B)　(C)

3. When will they contact you?
   (A)　(B)　(C)

found 設立する　beverage 飲料

Vocabulary, Grammar & Reading Comprehension

次の会話文を読んで下の問いに答えなさい。

スイスへの移住を考えている Hana は、スイスでの就職活動について友人の Geraldine に話を聞いています。

Hana: Why is there no written examination in the recruiting process of Swiss companies?

Geraldine: That's probably because universities in Switzerland are very difficult to graduate from, and most companies (A) an academic (B) as evidence that applicants are qualified to work for them.

Hana: So what do applicants do instead of taking an exam?

Geraldine: Applicants send details of their educational achievements and (C) history, including part-time jobs and volunteer activities, to the companies hiring new (D). This document is called a Curriculum Vitae (CV) in Great Britain and in some other English-speaking countries. In the United States it's called a (E).

Hana: What A[need / to / they / else / do / do]?

Geraldine: Applicants also attach a cover letter explaining why they want the job, and what special qualities or talents they have. This is one of the most important and difficult parts of job-hunting in Switzerland. If the cover letter is poorly written, recruiters won't even read the CV.

Hana: I see… What sort of photo should I submit?

Geraldine: If a photograph is asked for, your photograph should create a good impression. Serious applicants will have their photo taken wearing a nice suit, B[even / taken / or / have / one] at a professional photography studio.

cover letter 同封物に付ける説明の手紙

問 1. 文中の（ A ）から（ E ）に入れるのに最も適当なものを下からそれぞれ選びなさい。

employment   résumé   regard   employees   degree

問 2. 文中の A、B の [ ] 内の語を正しい順番に並べ替えて意味が通るようにしなさい。

A _____
B _____

問 3. 下の 1.〜 3. の英文が会話の内容に合っていれば T、間違っていれば F を選びなさい。

1. T F　Though Swiss universities are very difficult to enter, you don't have to take a written entrance exam.
2. T F　A CV includes a brief outline of your personal history, and is not as important as a résumé.
3. T F　A cover letter should be carefully written, since it is what recruiters read first.

TOEIC Reading Practice & Vocabulary

次の英文を読んで下の問に答えなさい。

Many Swiss high school graduates study at a higher technical school instead of going to a university. Switzerland has more than one hundred higher technical schools offering vocational training programs. Upon completion of one of these programs, students obtain a Professional Education and Training, or PET College Degree. Another alternative is to take a national exam to acquire a PET Diploma for more than 150 professions. Students with a Federal PET Diploma are allowed to sit exams for the more prestigious qualification, the Advanced Federal PET Diploma. In many countries, training for equivalent qualifications is achieved at university. Students who choose to go to university should not be content to graduate; it's recommended that they go on to study postgraduate courses and obtain a master's degree, which may help them find a better job. Additionally, some students take English proficiency tests such as TOEFL and Cambridge ESOL Examinations, to certify their English language proficiency. In Switzerland, TOEIC is not as popular as it is in Japan.

---

postgraduate 大学院の　**Cambridge ESOL Examinations** ケンブリッジ英語検定。ESOL (English for Speakers of Other Languages)

Unit 4

問1. 本文の内容に合うように、(A)〜(D)の中から最も適当なものを選びなさい。

1. Swiss students -------.
    (A) have few choices in higher vocational education
    (B) can't get qualifications or diplomas at technical schools
    (C) are expected to have the skills to become a professional engineer
    (D) can take some professional training at national institutions

2. The Advanced Federal PET Diploma -------.
    (A) is a qualification obtained by completing an undergraduate program
    (B) plays an important role in pre-school education
    (C) is more challenging than the Federal PET Diploma
    (D) is a type of compulsory education

3. In Switzerland, -------.
    (A) it's recommended that university students attend graduate school
    (B) you may not find a good job if you graduate from a Swiss university
    (C) you have to go to university if you want to get a job
    (D) vocational schools are not as popular as universities

4. As for English proficiency tests, -------.
    (A) the Federal PET Diploma examination is widely recognized
    (B) you may want to take an exam to prove your English ability
    (C) TOEIC is as popular an exam in Switzerland as it is in Japan
    (D) the cantons are responsible for regulating them

問2. 次の定義が意味する語（句）を本文中から選びなさい。
1. satisfied (   )
2. relating to a course of study undertaken after completing a (   )
   first degree
3. a certificate showing that you have completed a course (   )
   of study
4. studying or dealing with a school subject at a difficult level (   )
5. one of two or more available possibilities (   )

21

Unit 5
FINLAND

フィンランドでは若者による起業が盛んです。ここでは Rovio という会社をとりあげます。

Listening Practice 10

次の出だし英文を読んでから、そのあとに流れる英文を聴き、1.～3.の問いに適当な答えを (A)～(C) より選びなさい。

> Rovio is an entertainment media company in Finland, founded by three students from Helsinki University of Technology in 2003, as a mobile game development studio.

1. What is the name of the game?
   (A)　　(B)　　(C)

2. What is the platform for the game?
   (A)　　(B)　　(C)

3. How many times has the game been downloaded so far?
   (A)　　(B)　　(C)

Vocabulary, Grammar & Reading Comprehension

次の会話文を読んで下の問いに答えなさい。

日本の大学で経営学を学ぶReikoは、卒業後フィンランドで働きたいと思っています。そこで、フィンランドからの留学生Pirjoに相談しています。

Reiko: My friend has started a travel agency in the (A) area of Helsinki and she has ᴬ[me / asked / to / go / Finland / to] to join her business after finishing university. I am really interested in joint management with her. My Finnish language skills are not so poor but I need to (B) for business use.

Pirjo: Reiko, I have good news for you. One of the Helsinki University Summer School programmes provides a course which is intended for foreign students who are interested in studying entrepreneurship in Finland.

Reiko: That's unbelievable! You mean the course is suitable for students who want to improve their skills in entrepreneurship as well as in their Finnish language skills.

Pirjo: Exactly! Both of these skills will be developed during this course. The language of instruction is simplified Finnish. Business course content is (C) with Finnish language instruction. And it's OK to (D) the programme on their web page.

Reiko: That's perfect! I am ᴮ[participate in / more / curious / than / to] the programme. I am going to apply for the course as soon as possible.

Pirjo: You are (E) to write a 500 word introduction in the Finnish language. I'll proofread your application if you'd like. Let me know when you finish writing it.

joint management 共同経営　entrepreneurship 企業家であること

問 1. 文中の（A）から（E）に入れるのに最も適当なものを下からそれぞれ選びなさい。

improve　　surrounding　　required　　apply for　　facilitated

問 2. 文中のA、Bの[ ]内の語を正しい順番に並べ替えて意味が通るようにしなさい。

A _____

B _____

問 3. 下の 1.～ 3. の英文が会話の内容に合っていれば T、間違っていれば F を選びなさい。

1. T F   Reiko's friend wants her to join her business.
2. T F   Pirjo suggests that Reiko should join the programme, where she must study with Finnish students.
3. T F   In the programme course contents are taught in English.

TOEIC Reading Practice & Vocabulary

次の英文を読んで下の問に答えなさい。

In 2009 Finland was ranked in the 6th in the world in TOEFL iBT, while Japan was ranked lowest in Asia. Finnish is a language that is considerably different from English, as Japanese also is from English. So, why is English language education in Finland excellent? One reason may include an effect of such factors as economic and cultural globalization, the development of information and communication technology, and transnational cultural flows. Within this globalized society the number of transnational companies has been increasing and accordingly the role of English as lingua franca of business is further strengthened. For example, some Finnish and Nordic companies such as Nokia and Nordea choose English as their intra-corporate language.

Globalization has been progressing on a household-level language use. To take one example, the westernization of society has made it possible for Finnish broadcasting companies to acquire films and TV series in English. These same companies have made the decision to choose subtitling rather than dubbing – thus granting Finns unmediated exposure to English on a daily basis. This means that Finnish people have been able to listen to the English spoken on TV as it is spoken in the characters' countries of origin. English programmes have provided an informal way of learning English, in the same way as the Internet presents opportunities for language learning.

household-level 一般家庭的（日常的）なレベル　westernization 西洋化　subtitle （映画などに）字幕を付ける　exposure to English 英語に触れること

問 1. 本文の内容に合うように、(A)～(D) の中から最も適当なものを選びなさい。

1. The Finnish language -------.
   (A) is very close to English in structure and vocabulary
   (B) is very close to Japanese in grammatical structure
   (C) is very different from English
   (D) is a cross between Japanese and English

2. English language education in Finland is excellent because -------.
   (A) they have good English teachers and English programmes
   (B) they begin to learn English when they are 9 years old
   (C) they live in a highly globalized society
   (D) they have advanced ICT programmes

3. "Lingua franca" is -------.
   (A) the language which is spoken in France
   (B) the language which is used between people whose native languages are different
   (C) the language which is commonly spoken in British colonies
   (D) the language which is commonly spoken in European countries

4. Choose the statement which is true.
   (A) Finnish people enjoy English films dubbed in their own language
   (B) English TV programmes provide a good opportunity to learn English listening skills
   (C) All companies in Finland have adopted English as their intra-corporate language
   (D) English TV programmes have been introduced to formal education as teaching materials

問 2. 次の定義が意味する語（句）を本文中から選びなさい。

1. commonly known, familiar, on a daily basis ( )
2. within a company or organization ( )
3. words that appear on the screen during a movie ( )
4. direct ( )
5. movie ( )

Unit 6
SWEDEN

北欧の家具デザインは有名ですが、ここではスウェーデン発祥の世界的なインテリアショップ IKEA を取り上げます。

Listening Practice 12

次の出だし英文を読んでから、そのあとに流れる英文を聴き、1.〜3. の問いに適当な答えを (A)〜(C) より選びなさい。

> IKEA, the world's largest furniture retailer, began as a shop selling Scandinavian-style home furnishings and housewares in Sweden in 1943. IKEA is an acronym of the initials of its founder Ingvar Kamprad's name, Elmtaryd, the farm where he was born, and his home village, Agunnaryd.

1. What is the most well-known feature of IKEA furniture?
   (A)   (B)   (C)

2. What age group is IKEA furniture especially popular among?
   (A)   (B)   (C)

3. Approximately how many countries have IKEA stores in 2013?
   (A)   (B)   (C)

furnishing 備え付け家具 housewares 家庭用品 acronym 頭字語

Vocabulary, Grammar & Reading Comprehension

次の会話文を読んで下の問いに答えなさい。

日本の大学で国際関係を学んでいる Yuriko は、来週の授業でスウェーデンの就職状況について発表することになっています。そこで、スウェーデンからの留学生 Erik にいくつかの質問をしています。

Yuriko: My class, "Cross-cultural Understanding," A[us / to / a presentation / give / requires] concerning the working conditions in a foreign country. Next week it's my turn, and I'm going to talk about Sweden.

Erik: Sweden is famous for being a welfare state, and has traditionally had a broad range of publicly (A) income support, as well as health care and social services. Also, our country has widely-adopted measures called "Active Labor Market Policies, ALMPs," which are programs where the government is positively involved in getting (B) people back to work through training and work experience via temporary jobs.

Yuriko: That sounds interesting. Working in such an environment is also attractive for a foreigner like me.

Erik: Sweden has traditionally had an open-door immigration policy. Specific jobs (C) engineering and the IT fields often recruit foreign employees.

Yuriko: I am (D) in information processing, and am thinking of working in Sweden.

Erik: If that's your plan, I recommended you study Swedish. Since the general level of English is high in Sweden, speaking English will not give you much of an (E) over Swedes. You might also B[regions / going / less / to / populated / consider] such as northern Sweden, where the demand for skilled workers is higher. However, you should consider the harsh climate, and the long dark winter nights in Sweden before you make a decision to live there.

Yukiko: I take back what I just said, because I don't like cold weather nor the dark.

---

via 〜による、〜を通した　harsh 過酷な、厳しい

問 1. 文中の（ A ）から（ E ）に入れるのに最も適当なものを下からそれぞれ選びなさい。

| advantage | qualified | unemployed | provided | relating to |

問 2. 文中の A、B の [ ] 内の語を正しい順番に並べ替えて意味が通るようにしなさい。

A _____

B _____

問 3. 下の 1. ～ 3. の英文が会話の内容に合っていれば T、間違っていれば F を選びなさい。

1. T F Yuriko will probably move to Sweden in the near future.
2. T F Being fluent in English greatly works to an immigrant's advantage when applying for a job in Sweden.
3. T F The labor market in Sweden is open to immigrants.

TOEIC Reading Practice & Vocabulary

次の英文を読んで下の問に答えなさい。

Since 1993, Sweden has had a trade surplus with Japan, except in 2008. The main export items from Japan to Sweden are machinery, cars and chemical goods, while the main import items from Sweden are communication equipment, wood products and pharmaceuticals. In 2011, exports to Japan amounted to more than 15 billion SEK, Swedish Krona. Japan ranks as Sweden's fifth largest export market outside of Europe.

Swedish people also have heightened their interest in Japan, not only in its economy, but also in the areas of history and culture. The Stockholm School of Economics established The European Institute of Japanese Studies, EIJS, in 1992. The Institute contributes to the promotion of various research activities on Japan, holds seminars and lectures on Japan-related subjects, and opened a liaison office in Tokyo in 1997. Also, since 1999, students from the Stockholm School of Economics have held an annual collaborative project called "Exchange Japan" with students from Sweden's Royal Institute of Technology and Hitotsubashi University, in order to foster cultural and professional exchange between the two countries. Today, research on Japan is conducted at Stockholm University and at other institutes. Both economic and cultural exchanges between Sweden and Japan have been steadily increasing.

pharmaceutical 製薬　SEK スウェーデン クローナ（スウェーデン通貨）　Stockholm School of Economics ストックホルム商科大学　The European Institute of Japanese Studies 欧州日本研究所　liaison office 連絡事務所　Royal Institute of Technology スウェーデン王立工科大学

Unit 6

問1. 本文の内容に合うように、(A)〜(D)の中から最も適当なものを選びなさい。

1. ------- are major imports from Sweden to Japan.

   (A) Apparel and sports equipment
   (B) Automobiles and organic compounds
   (C) Furniture and pharmaceuticals
   (D) Mobile phones and video equipment

2. Japan -------.

   (A) has become Sweden's fifth-ranked trade partner in the world
   (B) has had a trade surplus with Sweden since 1993
   (C) generally imports more items than Sweden does from Japan
   (D) has balanced trade with Sweden

3. EIJS -------.

   (A) was founded in Stockholm in 1992
   (B) was organized as a department of Stockholm University
   (C) is the abbreviation for the Stockholm School of Economics
   (D) is the only research center on Japan in Sweden

4. "Exchange Japan" -------.

   (A) is held every other year
   (B) is an international project consisting mainly of university teachers
   (C) is organized with the goal of fostering economic exchange between Sweden and Japan
   (D) is a student activity forum at three universities in Japan and Sweden

問2. 次の定義が意味する語（句）を本文中から選びなさい。

1. being more than or in excess of what is needed or required (   )
2. relating to the production and sale of drugs and medicine (   )
3. occuring once every year (   )
4. communication or cooperation which facilitates a close working relationship between people or organizations (   )
5. activity that supports or encourages a cause, venture, or aim (   )

29

Unit 7
RUSSIA

ロシア人学生の就職先としては、天然ガスの生産・供給をおこなう世界最大級のエネルギー企業、ガスプロムに人気が集まります。

Listening Practice 14

次の出だし英文を読んでから、そのあとに流れる英文を聴き、1. ～ 3. の問いに適当な答えを (A) ～ (C) より選びなさい。

Gazprom, a major energy company in Russia, is especially popular with new university graduates as a future place of employment.

1. When was Gazprom established?
   (A)   (B)   (C)

2. What percentage of Russia's GNP is represented by Gazprom's production?
   (A)   (B)   (C)

3. What does Gazprom consider to be most important these days?
   (A)   (B)   (C)

30

Vocabulary, Grammar & Reading Comprehension

次の会話文を読んで下の問いに答えなさい。

ロシアで学ぶ日本人留学生の Kanako がロシア人学生の Yuri と将来の就職先について話しています。

Kanako: Which company do you have in (A) as your future prospective place of employment?

Yuri: Well, I think I would like to work at a foreign company here in Moscow, such as Toyota or BMW, since I like automobiles.

Kanako: Now I understand ᴬ[learning / speak / been / why / to / you've] Japanese and German.

Yuri: In fact, many students in Russia want to work at large-scale companies which were (B) established as state companies, such as Gazprom and LUKOIL. My parents also want me to work at such companies. At the same time, a certain number of students now want to work at foreign companies in Russia.

Kanako: That is what we call the onset of borderless job hunting ᴮ[to / Japan / is / popular / which / become / in / starting], too. However, most Japanese students don't seem to (C) that trend. I'm afraid many Japanese young people, including myself, are a little too timid.

Yuri: That's a (D)! I think working at foreign companies is fun, and also gives you an opportunity to (E) your outlook.

---

prospective 将来の　LUKOIL ルクオイル、ロシア最大の石油会社　onset 始まり　timid 内気な

問 1. 文中の（ A ）から（ E ）に入れるのに最も適当なものを下からそれぞれ選びなさい。

　　　broaden　　mind　　originally　　pity　　welcome

問 2. 文中のA、Bの[ ]内の語を正しい順番に並べ替えて意味が通るようにしなさい。

A _____

B _____

問3. 下の 1.～3. の英文が会話の内容に合っていれば T、間違っていれば F を選びなさい。

1. T F Yuri is planning to work for an automobile company outside of Russia.
2. T F Huge Russian companies are still more popular than foreign companies among Russian students.
3. T F Kanako is willing to work at a foreign company.

TOEIC Reading Practice & Vocabulary

次の英文を読んで下の問に答えなさい。

One of the most popular examinations among Russian university students is the Cambridge ESOL Examination. "ESOL" stands for "English for Speakers of Other Languages." The biggest reason for its popularity is that many Russian students are trying to get jobs at foreign companies both at home and abroad, and also because this examination is regarded, by companies such as IBM, Microsoft, Sony and Nokia, as an international standard for measuring the examinees' English language communication skills. However, it is not the only skill measured by the examination. The Cambridge ESOL Examination also measures the examinees' business abilities including business negotiation skills. Among other defining features of the examination is the length of time required for it. This examination takes as long as six hours because it measures the examinees' comprehensive English skills: reading, writing, listening and speaking. It is no wonder it's considered to be a very difficult examination by Russian students. However, they never run from it. They know that this tedious examination is worth their strenuous effort.

at home 国内で   strenuous たゆまない、精力的な

問1. 本文の内容に合うように、(A)〜(D) の中から最も適当なものを選びなさい。

1. The Cambridge ESOL Examination is -------.
    (A) for those whose native language is English
    (B) for those who study Russian at Cambridge University
    (C) for those who study Russian in order to enter Cambridge University
    (D) for those who speak English as a foreign language

2. The Cambridge ESOL Examination measures an -------.
    (A) examinees' academic skills
    (B) examinees' practical skills
    (C) examinees' creative skills
    (D) examinees' financial skills

3. Many Russian students who take the Cambridge ESOL Examination want jobs at foreign companies -------.
    (A) only in Russia
    (B) in Cambridge, England
    (C) inside and outside of Russia
    (D) only in countries outside of Russia

4. Although the Cambridge ESOL Examination is tiring, the Russian students don't -------.
    (A) hesitate to take it
    (B) decide to take it
    (C) welcome taking it
    (D) consider taking it

問2. 次の定義が意味する語（句）を本文中から選びなさい。

1. to judge the importance, value or effect of something　　（　　　　　）
2. formal discussion between people who are trying to reach an agreement　　（　　　　　）
3. to need something　　（　　　　　）
4. something important, interesting or typical of something　　（　　　　　）
5. showing great energy and determination　　（　　　　　）

Unit 8
SOUTH KOREA

ここでは韓国の財閥 (*Chaebol*)・サムスングループの中核企業で今や韓国を代表するグローバルカンパニーであるサムスン電子を取り上げます。

Listening Practice 🎧 16

次の出だし英文を読んでから、そのあとに流れる英文を聴き、1.〜3.の問いに適当な答えを (A)〜(C) より選びなさい。

> Samsung Electronics Co., Ltd. is the flagship enterprise of Samsung Group, a gigantic South Korean *Chaebol*, or type of South Korean business conglomerate, which includes companies such as LG Corp., SK Group, and Hyundai.

1. What does Samsung manufacture?
   (A)　　(B)　　(C)

2. How many new university graduates did Samsung hire in 2011?
   (A)　　(B)　　(C)

3. Why is Samsung the most desirable workplace among Korean college students?
   (A)　　(B)　　(C)

---

flagship 主力会社　**Chaebol** 韓国の財閥　**conglomerate** 巨大複合企業　**LG group** Lucky Goldstar (ラッキー金星) グループ。家電生産、コンビニ、建設業、精油などを経営する　**SK group** Sun Kyung グループ。石油精製や通信事業を基軸に展開する　**Hyundai** 重工業や自動車産業を基軸に展開する

Vocabulary, Grammar & Reading Comprehension

次の会話文を読んで下の問いに答えなさい。

ナオミは韓国人留学生 Min Ho に韓国の徴兵制度 (military conscription system) について尋ねています。

Naomi: The newspaper says that Taiwan is in a transitional (A) to end the country's military conscription system. They will have an all-volunteer military by the end of 2014. What about your country?

Min Ho: There are many countries which have a military conscription system. South Korea has a system obligating all male citizens to join the military. Finland is another country that requires mandatory military service.

Naomi: I've never heard of that. It means (B) military service for men, doesn't it? Japan doesn't have (B) military service. All members of Japan's Self-Defense Forces are volunteers. How do they enter the military in South Korea?

Min Ho: All male citizens 18 years of age ᴬ[to / examination / are / undergo / an / obligated] for the military within a year. They need to conduct several tests, a including a psychological test, a physical examination, (C) test, and so on. All males at the age of 20 serve mandatory military service, except those who are (D) because of some medical condition.

Naomi: How long do they serve? Do they go to college after they complete military service? Can they change the date of their enlistment? Can they delay military service?

Min Ho: They serve approximately two years. They say that people may obtain a deferment, if they're between 20 and 28 years old and are college students, for example. However, there are some exceptions. Now a lot of young Korean males enter university after taking military aptitude tests, then they ᴮ[temporary / school / leave / a / from / take] to serve in the army. After finishing military duty, they return to school and (E) their studies.

---

mandatory 強制的な　Self Defense Force 自衛隊　physical examination 身体検査　enlistment 入隊
deferment 兵役猶予　aptitude test 適性検査

問 1. 文中の（ A ）から（ E ）に入れるのに最も適当なものを下からそれぞれ選びなさい。

| an aptitude | exempt | mandatory | phase | resume |

問 2. 文中の A、B の [ ] 内の語を正しい順番に並べ替えて意味が通るようにしなさい。

A _____

B _____

35

問3. 下の1.～3.の英文が会話の内容に合っていればT、間違っていればFを選びなさい。

1. T F　Taiwan introduced a dual conscription and volunteer military system in 2014.
2. T F　People call a person who serves mandatory military service a "volunteer."
3. T F　The average age of Koreans who graduate from college is higher than that of Japanese.

TOEIC Reading Practice & Vocabulary

次の英文を読んで下の問に答えなさい。

The Test of English for International Communication, or TOEIC, is the English language proficiency test which is most frequently taken in Japan and South Korea. The average TOEIC score is 626 points in South Korea, which is much higher than Japan's average score of 510 points. According to the results of a survey, almost 100 percent of South Korean companies ask to look at potential employees' TOEIC scores. By comparison, just 83.4 percent of Japan's companies require TOEIC scores. Leading companies in South Korea require an average TOEIC score of 700 points. Samsung requires a score over 900 points. Japan's Panasonic Corporation also requires a score which exceeds 900 points. However, many Japanese companies do not require applicants to achieve high scores, compared to South Korean companies.

Moreover, some top South Korean companies have started holding internal meetings in English, and require employees to write email and documents in English. That's why Korean students, even those scoring around 870 points, worry about their scores and study hard to improve them. In fact, 870 points is equivalent to an "A" grade, which means that a person is capable of communicating sufficiently in English as a non-native speaker. Recently, a lot of Koreans aim for perfect scores on their TOEIC exams.

leading company　一流会社　　internal meeting　社内ミーティング

問1. 本文の内容に合うように、(A)～(D)の中から最も適当なものを選びなさい。

1. According to the passage, TOEIC is -------.
   (A) held in over 80 percent of Japanese companies, with up to fourteen tests a year
   (B) generally offered for free in South Korea
   (C) a test only for non-native speakers of English living in Japan and South Korea
   (D) required by many Japanese and South Korean companies

2. According to the passage, -------.
   (A) Japan's average TOEIC scores are much higher than South Korea's
   (B) average TOEIC scores in South Korea are higher than those in Japan
   (C) Japanese and Chinese test takers can take the test as many times as they'd like
   (D) South Korea has the highest average TOEIC scores in the world.

3. According to the passage, companies in South Korea -------.
   (A) place greater significance on TOEIC scores than Japanese companies
   (B) do not place much significance on TOEIC scores, because almost all South Korean applicants have high scores
   (C) believe that the most important requirement for applicants is to obtain high TOEIC scores.
   (D) consider TOEIC to be the best English aptitude test

4. According to the passage, -------.
   (A) a lot of South Korean applicants are satisfied with TOEIC scores above 900
   (B) no Japanese companies hold internal meetings in English
   (C) most Japanese companies require prospective employees to have TOEIC scores as high as those required by South Korean companies such as Samsung
   (D) few Japanese companies require applicants to achieve very high TOEIC scores

問 2. 次の定義が意味する語（句）を本文中から選びなさい。
1. questions you ask a certain number of people in order to determine their opinions　　(　　　　)
2. a piece of paper that contains official information　　(　　　　)
3. enough, as much as you need　　(　　　　)
4. be able to, or can　　(　　　　)
5. a big company, or a group of companies　　(　　　　)

Unit 9
VIETNAM

ベトナムでは、国際企業への就職を希望する学生が多いですが、必ずしも国内企業に人気が無いわけではありません。ここでは Vinamilk というベトナム国内の企業を紹介します。

Listening Practice 🎧 18

次の出だし英文を読んでから、そのあとに流れる英文を聴き、1.～3. の問いに適当な答えを (A)～(C) より選びなさい。

> A growing number of Vietnamese college students dream of working for an international company after graduation. They believe that working in an international company would be more beneficial to them than working for a traditional Vietnamese company.

1. What type of company is Vinamilk?
   (A)   (B)   (C)

2. What is the percentage of Vinamilk's domestic market share?
   (A)   (B)   (C)

3. Why is Vinamilk popular with students?
   (A)   (B)   (C)

Vocabulary, Grammar & Reading Comprehension

次の会話文を読んで下の問いに答えなさい。

日本の大学で情報社会学を専攻する Shota は国際企業に就職したいと考えています。そこで、友人である Loan にベトナム学生の就職事情を聞いています。

Shota: Hi, Loan. Thank you for inviting me to your party, but I'm (A) I can't go. I'm really busy every day with job interviews and orientation sessions held here and there. I think it would be great if I could work for an international company, but I suppose it would be very (B) to do so. Are international companies popular with Vietnamese students?

Loan: Hmm, recently there is a growing number of students who ᴬ[dream / an / for / working / of] international company. They seem to think that the work environment, wages and (C) provided at international companies are good. However, some domestic companies such as Vinamilk are also popular, because they are globally-competitive, and offer good working conditions.

Shota: Oh, I know that company. That's Vietnam's largest dairy company, which holds a large domestic (D) share, right?

Loan: That's right! Large companies such as Vinamilk hold campus recruiting programs at Vietnam's top universities.

Shota: What are campus recruiting programs? Are they a type of training course for job seekers?

Loan: Sort of. Recruiting programs offer students an opportunity to learn more about available vocations, and offer them a chance to develop their (E). Of course, these programs give companies a chance to recruit good students. That ᴮ[for / both / good / parties / is].

---

domestic 国内の　dairy 乳製品　sort of まあね（会話表現）

問 1. 文中の（ A ）から（ E ）に入れるのに最も適当なものを下からそれぞれ選びなさい。

> market　　careers　　competitive　　afraid　　benefits

問 2. 文中のA、Bの [ ] 内の語を正しい順番に並べ替えて意味が通るようにしなさい。

A _____

B _____

問 3. 下の 1.〜3. の英文が会話の内容に合っていれば T、間違っていれば F を選びなさい。

1. T F   Shota wants to work for a foreign company.
2. T F   Vinamilk is a Vietnamese dairy company with a small domestic market share.
3. T F   Students may be offered jobs through campus recruiting programs.

TOEIC Reading Practice & Vocabulary

次の英文を読んで下の問に答えなさい。

A bachelor's degree is given to graduates who finish four-to-six year programs at universities or colleges in Vietnam. It takes four years for students studying social science; five years for students of industrial engineering, and six years for students majoring in medical and dental sciences. Since only 15% or less of Vietnamese high school graduates go on to attend university or college, graduates who have bachelor's degrees are in an extremely advantageous position for job-hunting in Vietnam. They are on the career track, and are good candidates for executive positions in the future. Most graduates who have bachelor's degrees are conscious of their elite status, and they take an uncompromising attitude toward finding the right job. Because of this, it's not unusual for graduates to take part-time jobs until they find a satisfying and worthwhile job.

industrial engineering 生産工学   career track 出世コース   executive position 管理職
uncompromising 断固とした

問 1. 本文の内容に合うように、(A)〜(D) の中から最も適当なものを選びなさい。

1. University students receive bachelor's degrees -------.
    (A) when entering a university or college
    (B) only if they major in social science
    (C) after completing a several-year program at a university or college
    (D) from people who have graduated from a university

2. The ratio of Vietnamese students advancing to university or college -------.
   (A) is extremely high
   (B) has not been determined
   (C) proves that 15% of all the universities in Vietnam are national ones
   (D) is less than one-fifth of high school graduates

3. Graduates from university or college -------.
   (A) have great advantages when job-hunting
   (B) find it difficult to get a job because they have no social skills
   (C) can avoid problems associated with job hunting in the future
   (D) do not need to seek employment

4. Some university graduates believe that -------.
   (A) it's better to work part-time than to take an unfulfilling job
   (B) universities and colleges should give bachelor's degrees only to elite students
   (C) the first impression they give can make or break them at a job interview
   (D) working part-time gives them more advantages in job hunting

問2. 次の定義が意味する語（句）を本文中から選びなさい。

1. a subject relating to the study of people in society   (   )
2. relating to your teeth   (   )
3. work involved in designing and building machines, roads, (   )
   bridges, etc.
4. a person running for office or applying for a job   (   )
5. a company manager who helps make important decisions   (   )

Unit 10
CHINA

中国人学生の就職先としては China Mobile Limited のような大企業が人気を博しています。

Listening Practice　CD 20

次の出だし英文を読んでから、そのあとに流れる英文を聴き、1.～3. の問いに適当な答えを (A)～(C) より選びなさい。

> China Mobile Limited, one of the world's largest companies, is a Chinese state-owned telecommunications company, whose headquarters are in Hong Kong.

1. Which Stock Exchange is China Mobile listed on?
   (A)　(B)　(C)

2. How many people work at China Mobile and its subsidiaries?
   (A)　(B)　(C)

3. What news attracted global attention recently?
   (A)　(B)　(C)

Vocabulary, Grammar & Reading Comprehension

次の会話文を読んで下の問いに答えなさい。

日本の大学で学ぶ中国人留学生の Chun が就職活動を始めた日本人学生の Tadashi と日中の就職活動について話しています

Tadashi: Hi, Chun, it's nice to see you again.

Chun: Hello Tadashi! It's a surprise to see you in a (A) suit. Where are you going dressed all in black?

Tadashi: I'm going to a job interview. This is a Japanese-style interview suit. Japanese students wear them for interviews with (B) employers. Today is a very important day for me. That's why I'm dressed formally.

Chun: Well, I can't believe it. I don't think I would (C) a Japanese interview suit. I might feel very uncomfortable wearing one. In fact, I ᴬ**[attend / going / a / thought / were / you / to / funeral]** or something.

Tadashi: Oh, no. This is precisely what you wear to a job interview here in Japan. Isn't it the same in China? What do you wear to a job interview in China?

Chun: We go to job interviews in our (D) everyday clothes, such as jeans, a T-shirt and sneakers. In this way, a Chinese job ᴮ**[proceeds / a / in / friendly / interview]** manner. In fact, at some job interviews in China, interviewees are starting to (E) like Japanese students.

問 1. 文中の（A）から（E）に入れるのに最も適当なものを下からそれぞれ選びなさい。

casual   formal   dress   wear   prospective

問 2. 文中のA、Bの [ ] 内の語を正しい順番に並べ替えて意味が通るようにしなさい。

A _____
B _____

問 3. 下の 1.～3. の英文が会話の内容に合っていればT、間違っていればFを選びなさい。

1. T F Tadashi and Chun are acquaintances.
2. T F Chun doesn't like Japanese-style funerals because they are so formal.
3. T F Some Chinese job seekers wear formal clothing to job interviews.

TOEIC Reading Practice & Vocabulary

次の英文を読んで下の問に答えなさい。

In the PISA (Program for International Student Assessment) test of 2009, Chinese students from Shanghai ranked first in three subjects: reading, mathematics and science. This brilliant performance by Chinese students surprised everyone, since it was the first time for China to participate in the test, and nobody expected such an excellent outcome. Some say that China has emerged as a world power in the field of education, as well as in terms of economics. However, others criticize this broad statement as coming to a hasty conclusion. They insist that while it's true that Chinese students outscored their international peers on the test, the outstanding scores only represent a small number of elite students in Shanghai. Meanwhile, Japanese students ranked eighth in reading, ninth in mathematics, and fifth in science out of the sixty-five participating countries. This mediocre result for Japan, who scored first or second in math and science in 2000, is said to be due to the new "pressure-free education system" which was introduced in 2002. In conclusion, it's important that we teach our students in such a way that they may experience the joys of learning and of reading, which is the most fundamental educational skill for learning.

PISA OECDが実施する15歳を対象とする国際的な学習到達度調査　world power 世界的強国　in terms of ～　～の面で　broad 大雑把な　mediocre 平凡な　pressure-free education system ゆとり教育

問 1. 本文の内容に合うように、(A)～(D)の中から最も適当なものを選びなさい。

1. Chinese students' scores on the PISA test were number one in -------.
   (A) reading and mathematics
   (B) mathematics and science
   (C) reading and science
   (D) reading, mathematics and science

2. Some people do not agree that China is a world power in terms of education because -------.
   (A) test scores of Chinese students are uniform nationwide
   (B) test scores of Chinese students don't represent nationwide average scores
   (C) Shanghai is one of the largest cities in China
   (D) most students in Shanghai are very smart

3. Japan participated in the 2009 PISA test with ------- other countries.
   (A) 64
   (B) 65
   (C) 66
   (D) 67

4. What is true about the PISA test?
   (A) Japan outscored most European countries.
   (B) Japanese students' average scores were better than Chinese students' average scores.
   (C) China did not participate in the 2006 PISA test.
   (D) China will be No. 1 in the next PISA test as well.

問 2. 次の定義が意味する語（句）を本文中から選びなさい。

1. incredible or excellent (   )
2. to come out of something (   )
3. to talk about other people's faults (   )
4. people who are the same age as you, or of the same social class (   )
5. average, not very good (   )

Unit 11
THAILAND

サイアム・セメントは王室系企業で、タイ王室財産管理局が出資しています。2013年にはタイの大学生間で最も人気がある企業となりました。

Listening Practice 🎧 22

次の出だし英文を読んでから、そのあとに流れる英文を聴き、1.～3.の問いに適当な答えを (A)～(C) より選びなさい。

> The Siam Cement Group (SCG) is the largest industrial business conglomerate in Thailand.

1. How many people are working for SCG?
   (A)   (B)   (C)

2. When was the company established?
   (A)   (B)   (C)

3. What is the company not involved in?
   (A)   (B)   (C)

Vocabulary, Grammar & Reading Comprehension

次の会話文を読んで下の問いに答えなさい。

> 日本の大学で教育学を専攻する Tatsunori は卒業後タイで日本語を教えたいと考えています。そこで、タイ人留学生の Napaporn にタイの教育事情について質問しています。

Tatsunori: Hello, Napaporn! I am thinking of teaching Japanese in Bangkok after graduating from university. I read in yesterday's newspaper that Thai students are very interested in learning Japanese.

Napaporn: Oh that's a good idea. I've got the 2009 (A). They're a bit dated, but they show that slightly less than 80,000 students across Thailand studied Japanese, and that there were about 1,200 Japanese language teachers at that time. It was (B) that half of the students who studied Japanese were at the high school level.

Tatsunori: Do you know why studying Japanese is so popular in Thailand?

Napaporn: (C) it was the result of demands from Japanese companies which invested heavily in Thailand, and also ᴬ[due / growing / people / for / a / demand / to] who are proficient in the Japanese language.

Tatsunori: I'm very (D) to know how Japanese language learning was introduced to the educational context in Thailand. Do you know anything about that?

Napaporn: Oh, I know. Japanese language began to be taught in a (E) way around the 1960s, with support from the Japanese government. In 1965, Thammasat University began offering Japanese language courses. And in 1982, the university launched a ᴮ[majoring / the Japanese / in / programme / language].

---

a bit dated 少し古い　educational context 教育現場　Thammasat University タンマサート大学。バンコク市内にある名門大学。

問 1. 文中の（ A ）から（ E ）に入れるのに最も適当なものを下からそれぞれ選びなさい。

| curious | systematic | estimated | needless to say | statistics |

問 2. 文中の A、B の [ ] 内の語を正しい順番に並べ替えて意味が通るようにしなさい。

A _____

B _____

問 3.　下の 1.〜3. の英文が会話の内容に合っていれば T、間違っていれば F を選びなさい。

1. T F 　In Thailand, 1200 Japanese people taught Japanese language in 2009.
2. T F 　Most Japanese language learners were high school students in 2009.
3. T F 　The Japanese government offered support when Japanese language teaching programs started.

TOEIC Reading Practice & Vocabulary

次の英文を読んで下の問に答えなさい。

Thai people's average TOEFL iBT score was 75 in 2010. At the time Thailand ranked 116 out of a total of 163 countries. Of course, TOEFL scores are not representative of English proficiency of the overall Thai population, but the level of English proficiency was low in comparison with many Asian countries.

A number of factors which have contributed to the failure of English teaching-and-learning were examined in detail by researchers. Some say it is due to poorly motivated students, others say it is because of rare opportunities for students' exposure to English outside of the classroom. Most researchers, however, point out that the main cause for failure is unqualified and poorly-trained teachers. Actually, primary and secondary school teachers have heavy teaching loads, inadequately equipped classrooms, lack of education technology, and the university entrance examination system. But above all, most seriously, teachers don't have sufficient English language skills nor cultural knowledge.

Institutions of higher education understand this fact, and try to give assistance to teachers by organizing training sessions, seminars, and conferences. Some universities have been organizing professional development training courses for high school English teachers. Judging from the end-of-course evaluation surveys, teachers who participated in the course are satisfied with it.

TOEFL iBT TOEFL とは Test Of English as a Foreign Language（外国語としての英語テスト）のこと。iBT は internet Based Testing のことで、インターネットを利用した試験形式をとっている。120 点満点。 **teaching load** 授業の負担　**inadequately equipped** 授業環境が未整備の　**end-of-course** 授業終了後の **evaluation form** 授業評価用の書式

問 1. 本文の内容に合うように、(A) 〜 (D) の中から最も適当なものを選びなさい。

1. Thailand's 2010 TOEFL iBT scores -------.
   (A) were lower than most European countries, but a bit higher than those of other Asian countries
   (B) were the lowest of all the countries which participated in the test
   (C) were lower than most Asian countries
   (D) were not as low as they were expected to be

2. The major reason for the low scores was -------.
   (A) that the students are not motivated
   (B) that the students don't speak English in their everyday lives
   (C) that they don't have enough money to study English
   (D) that the quality of English teachers is low

3. ------- is NOT a problem facing primary and secondary school teachers in Thailand.
   (A) the university entrance exam system
   (B) a low salary
   (C) too much work
   (D) lack of education technology

4. English teachers are allowed to -------.
   (A) spend 6 months in any English speaking country to learn teaching skills
   (B) attend professional development training courses organized by universities
   (C) organize training sessions, seminars and conferences
   (D) teach small-sized classes

問 2. 次の定義が意味する語（句）を本文中から選びなさい。

1. everything in general　　　　　　　　　　　　　（　　　　　　）
2. affected by something or experiencing something　（　　　　　　）
3. help or support　　　　　　　　　　　　　　　　（　　　　　　）
4. a place where an organization takes care of people for a period of time　（　　　　　　）
5. to make someone willing to work or study hard to achieve something　（　　　　　　）

Unit 12
INDIA

Tata Motors は日本の自動車メーカー・スズキのインド法人 Multi Suzuki と並んでインドを代表する自動車会社です。

Listening Practice 24

次の出だし英文を読んでから、そのあとに流れる英文を聴き、1.～3. の問いに適当な答えを (A) ～ (C) より選びなさい。

Tata Motors is India's largest automobile manufacturing company.

1. What does Tata Motors produce?
   (A)　　(B)　　(C)

2. In which country has Tata Motors started a joint venture?
   (A)　　(B)　　(C)

3. What is Tata Motors focused on?
   (A)　　(B)　　(C)

Vocabulary, Grammar & Reading Comprehension

次の会話文を読んで下の問いに答えなさい。

日本の大学でヒンディー語を学ぶShinjiroは、インドのカースト制度についてレポートを書いています。そこで、インド人で日本の自動車会社で通訳者として働いている友人のNarendraに相談しています

Shinjiro: Hello Narendra, I'm writing a report about India's Caste System. I want to ask you some questions about it, okay? I know there are four different levels; Brahman, Kshatriya, Vaishya, and Shudra. Also, there is one more level called Harijans. Would you please tell me about Harijans?

Narendra: Yes, it refers to people who belong to the lowest level of the Caste System ᴬ[untouchables / as / *Dalits* / or / known]. The word "Harijan" (A) means "child of God". It was first used instead of *Dalits* by Mahatma Gandhi. He said it was (B) to call people 'untouchable; and called them *Harijans*.

Shinjiro: Do *Dalits* still have trouble finding jobs or acquiring a university education?

Narendra: They did a long time ago. But in 1950 the (C) government decided to (D) 22.5% of university placements and government jobs for *Dalits*. By 1993, that percentage doubled.

Shinjiro: As Indian markets become more globalized, ᴮ[will / a larger/ be / there / debate] over the country's 3,000-year-old Caste System.

Narendra: Yeah. That's right. I hope a more (E) approach will be taken to allow companies in India to recruit employees based on their talent, not on their Caste.

---

dalit 不可触賤民、カースト制度外にあって最も差別される人々　Mahatma Gandhi マハトマ・ガンディ (1869～1948)、インド独立の父

問 1. 文中の（ A ）から（ E ）に入れるのに最も適当なものを下からそれぞれ選びなさい。

　　　liberal　　reserve　　federal　　literally　　wrong

問 2. 文中のA、Bの[ ]内の語を正しい順番に並べ替えて意味が通るようにしなさい。

A _____
B _____

問 3. 下の 1.～3. の英文が会話の内容に合っていれば T、間違っていれば F を選びなさい。

1. T F　The word 'Dalit' is synonymous with untouchable.
2. T F　It is still impossible for Hajirans to find government jobs.
3. T F　Narendra hopes that in the future Indian companies will employ people based on their Caste.

TOEIC Reading Practice & Vocabulary

次の英文を読んで下の問に答えなさい。

The Japanese-Language Proficiency Test (JLPT), which has been offered by the Japan Foundation and Japan Educational Exchanges and Services organization since 1984, is regarded as a reliable means of evaluating and certifying the language proficiency of non-native Japanese speakers. In the city of Pune, which is located on the western edge of the Deccan plateau, the popularity of Japanese language learning is amazing. Vinay Sathe, coordinator of Japanese language course in Tilak Maharashtra University says that Pune has become a hub for Japanese learners in the last few years. According to him, as many as 5,000 students enroll in Japanese courses each year, though the drop-out rate is high. Around 100 students reached the advanced level, and, thus far, most of them have jobs in various Japanese companies as translators or interpreters. Since Japanese grammar and that of their local language is similar, the students find it easy to learn Japanese. Sathe says that some of the idioms and phrases used in the two languages are surprisingly similar.

The Japanese Language Proficiency Test　日本語能力試験　**Japan Foundation**　日本国際交流基金　**Japan Educational Exchanges and Service**　日本国際教育支援協会　**Pune**　プネ市、インド中西部の大都市、東のオックスフォードと呼ばれる学術都市。　**Tilak Maharashtra University**　プネにある大学、1921年設立。

問 1. 本文の内容に合うように、(A)～(D) の中から最も適当なものを選びなさい。

1. The JLPT is -------.
   (A) taken by foreign people living in Japan
   (B) a Japanese proficiency test for Japanese people
   (C) a reliable means to evaluate the language proficiency of native Japanese speakers
   (D) has been carried out since 1984

2. Pune is a city -------.

    (A) on the eastern edge of the Deccan Plateau

    (B) where a lot of Japanese people are living

    (C) where the Japanese language is commonly spoken

    (D) where many people are learning the Japanese language

3. Mr. Vinary Sathe says that -------.

    (A) Pune has been playing a central function in Japanese language learning

    (B) every year no less than 5000 students take Japanese courses in his university and most of them go on to the advanced level

    (C) many of the advanced-level students work as administrators in Japanese companies

    (D) Pune is so full of natural beauty that many people feel like learning Japanese language

4. Mr. Vinary Sathe says that it is easy for students in Pune to learn Japanese because -------.

    (A) it shares a lot of similarities with the language spoken throughout India

    (B) Japanese idioms share some similarities to those of their native language

    (C) they can easily find good jobs with Japanese companies

    (D) they have good Japanese teachers at their university

問 2. 次の定義が意味する語（句）を本文中から選びなさい。

1. to judge how good, useful, or successful something is   (   )
2. a way of doing or achieving something   (   )
3. a high or difficult level   (   )
4. someone who changes spoken words from one   (   )
   language into another
5. a person who leaves school before they have finished   (   )
   their studies

Unit 13
BRAZIL

Bug Agentes Biológicos は、それまでの殺虫剤にとって代わる画期的な害虫駆除方法を考案し、2013 年もっとも革新的な企業トップ 10 の最上位にランクされた会社です。その方法とは何でしょうか。

Listening Practice CD 26

次の出だし英文を読んでから、そのあとに流れる英文を聴き、1.～3.の問いに適当な答えを (A)～(C) より選びなさい。

Brazil is the world's largest consumer of chemical pesticides. Recently they're phasing out the more noxious chemical pesticides used by farmers.

1. How do wasps help farmers?
   (A)　　(B)　　(C)

2. How are wasps brought to the fields?
   (A)　　(B)　　(C)

3. How are wasps different from chemical pesticides?
   (A)　　(B)　　(C)

---

chemical pesticide 合成殺虫剤　phase out 段階的に廃止する　noxious 有毒な

54

Vocabulary, Grammar & Reading Comprehension

次の会話文を読んで下の問いに答えなさい。

大学の農学部で海外の農業事情を学ぶ Michiyo は、ブラジル人留学生 Eduard から自国の農業事情について聞いています。

Michiyo: Brazil is the fifth largest country in the world. Since it has a rich supply of natural (A) such as water, land and a favorable climate, it has a good chance of becoming the world's largest agricultural (B), and a major food supplier for the global marketplace.

Eduardo: That's right. Even now, my country supplies the entire world with most of the soybeans, corn, oranges, coffee, sugarcane, and other produce. Agriculture accounts for 25% of the nation's GDP; and 35% of Brazilans are employed in agriculture. It's a vital part of the Brazilian economy, ᴬ[is / agribusiness / and / so].

Michiyo: Oh yeah, that's exactly what I learned from today's lecture. However, I still don't understand the difference between agriculture and agribusiness.

Eduard: Oh, that's easy! Agriculture simply refers to crop production, while agribusiness more (C) includes seed supply, agrichemicals, farm machinery production, food processing, marketing, and retailing.

Michiyo: Are biofuels part of agribusiness?

Eduard: Yeah! Biofuels are gaining more public and scientific acclaim, ᴮ[concern / as / increases / about global warming]. The increase in popularity of biofuel is driven by factors such as oil price, the need for increased energy security, concern over greenhouse gas (D) from (E) fuels, and support via government subsidies.

---

account for 割合を占める　**agrichemical** 農薬　**retail** 小売する　**biofuel** 生物燃料　**acclaim** 絶賛　**subsidy** 助成金、補助金

問 1. 文中の（ A ）から（ E ）に入れるのに最も適当なものを下からそれぞれ選びなさい。

　　resources　　comprehensively　　fossil　　emissions　　superpower

問 2. 文中の A、B の [ ] 内の語を正しい順番に並べ替えて意味が通るようにしなさい。

A _____

B _____

問 3. 下の 1.～3. の英文が会話の内容に合っていれば T、間違っていれば F を選びなさい。

1. T F   35% of Brazilians are employed in the agriculture business.
2. T F   Coal mining is part of agribusiness.
3. T F   Brazil supplies 25% of the world's agricultural crops.

TOEIC Reading Practice & Vocabulary

次の英文を読んで下の問に答えなさい。

Brazil has only five of the top 500 universities in the world. This is partly because a very small number of degree programs are offered in English. Brazilian universities should consider offering more courses in English, but they have historically resisted introducing English as the instruction language. Some people fear that teaching in English rather than Portuguese would threaten Brazil's national identity.

Another objection is that teaching in English would turn the already elite Brazilian universities even more elite. That might be the case if they gave up teaching in Portuguese altogether. However, the coexistence of courses in English and Portuguese provide Brazilian students with opportunities to socialize with foreigners, and improve their proficiency in English. Generally, students prefer to attend universities where classes are taught in English. The first steps for an effective internationalization of Brazil's higher education system have already been taken. University teachers are required to publish more materials in English. Academic publications in English reach a much larger audience, and have more impact on the world's scientific and cultural development.

instruction language 授業中使用する言語   national sovereignty 国家の主権   socialize ～と付き合う
academic publication 学術出版物

問 1. 本文の内容に合うように、(A)～(D)の中から最も適当なものを選びなさい。

1. In Brazil most university classes are not taught in English because -------.
   (A) some Brazilians believe they may lose their national identity if classes are conducted in English
   (B) they don't like studying English at school
   (C) they don't like America
   (D) there are almost no British students in Brazil

2. Some Brazilians fear that if university classes are conducted in English, -------.
   (A) students will stop learning Portuguese
   (B) students may think English is more important than Portuguese
   (C) there would be a wider gap between good and bad universities
   (D) students would leave Brazil to study in English-speaking countries

3. If classes are conducted both in English and Portuguese, -------.
   (A) the number of British and American students will increase
   (B) students will have more opportunities to make friends with foreign students
   (C) students will have poor English proficiency
   (D) students don't have to go to English-speaking countries

4. University teachers are required to -------.
   (A) publish papers and essays in English
   (B) go to foreign countries for academic presentations
   (C) teach their students in English
   (D) invite foreign students to their classes, and socialize with them

問 2. 次の定義が意味する語（句）を本文中から選びなさい。

1. the qualification obtained by students who have completed a university course (   )
2. to spend time with other people (   )
3. being together in the same place at the same time (   )
4. a powerful effect that something has on somebody or something (   )
5. books, magazines, and other reading materials (   )

Unit 14
THE UNITED STATES

日本でもおなじみのコカコーラの起源は1886年にまでさかのぼります。

Listening Practice 🎧 28

次の出だし英文を読んでから、そのあとに流れる英文を聴き、1.〜3.の問いに適当な答えを (A)〜(C) より選びなさい。

> Coca-Cola was created in 1886 by physician John S. Pemberton as a headache and stomachache remedy.

1. Where was Coca-Cola first sold?
   (A)　(B)　(C)

2. What ingredient did Coca-Cola originally contain?
   (A)　(B)　(C)

3. Where is the recipe for Coca-Cola kept?
   (A)　(B)　(C)

remedy 治療法　ingredient 成分

Vocabulary, Grammar & Reading Comprehension

次の会話文を読んで下の問いに答えなさい。

アメリカの大学で経営学を専攻する Hiroshi は、友人の Marty がどのようにして Intel に就職したかを聞いています。

Hiroshi: I hear you already (A) a nice engineering position at Intel starting next year. That's a great company to work for. How did you (B) that?

Marty: Actually, it was quite easy. Last summer I had an internship at their manufacturing plant near our campus. I got along well with everyone and really liked the working atmosphere, so I told my boss I was interested in working there. He asked to see my résumé, and a copy of my college (C). He helped me get hired.

Hiroshi: Wow! That's hard to believe. Can anyone who interns for them get a job there?

Marty: No, don't be silly. The purpose of internships is to search for (D) employees. The company looks for recruits ᴬ[who / to / seem / fit in well / their team / with] and who share the same goals and visions as the company. Actually, most interns don't get hired.

Hiroshi: I see. I've noticed that many American companies are interested in (E) a potential employee's school transcripts. In Japan, most companies don't care about university grades as ᴮ[has / the / long / candidate / as / graduated].

Marty: Really? In the US, employers believe good grades indicate that a candidate will most likely be a hard-working employee.

---

internship 実習訓練期間、見習い期間　intern 実習生として働く　potential employee 従業員になる見込みがある人　school transcript 成績証明書

問1. 文中の（A）から（E）に入れるのに最も適当なものを下からそれぞれ選びなさい。

　　potential　　manage　　landed　　viewing　　transcripts

問2. 文中のA、Bの[ ]内の語を正しい順番に並べ替えて意味が通るようにしなさい。

A _____
B _____

問 3. 下の 1.〜3. の英文が会話の内容に合っていれば T、間違っていれば F を選びなさい。

1. T F　Marty will begin working as an engineer at Intel this summer.
2. T F　The place where Marty worked as an intern is far from the university campus.
3. T F　The boss thought that Marty would be an asset to the company.

TOEIC Reading Practice & Vocabulary

次の英文を読んで下の問に答えなさい。

The Scholastic Assessment Test, or SAT, is an entrance examination that is used in the United States by most colleges and universities, to help make admissions decisions. The idea is to provide colleges with one common criterion that can be used to compare all applicants. However, the SAT is just one factor in the admissions decision process. Schools also consider an individual's high school or college grade point average (GPA), academic transcripts, letters of recommendation, interviews and personal essays. In fact, there are many students who never take the SAT. The way these students enter a university is by first applying as a part-time student. Since most universities allow part-time status to all applicants, individuals may easily enroll in one or two classes. Then, if their grades are sufficient, the university will allow them to enroll full time. However, full or part-time students who do not maintain adequate grades may lose their status. And, if their grades do not improve, the university will suspend them from school. In many cases, these students may not be able to enroll in the same school again. Because of this, students in American universities must work hard to complete their degrees, and many do not graduate.

　　　SAT 大学進学適性試験、米国で大学進学時の要件として広く用いられる試験　**criterion** 基準
　　　admissions decision process 入学許可決定プロセス　**GPA** 学業成績平均値　**status** 地位

Unit 14

問 1. 本文の内容に合うように、(A)～(D)の中から最も適当なものを選びなさい。

1. The SAT is a(n) -------.
   (A) test required for all students who want to apply for a college or university
   (B) the sole factor in deciding whether a student may enter a college or university
   (C) official application form required for applying to a college or university
   (D) test that is generally, but not always taken by college and university applicants

2. The purpose of the SAT is -------.
   (A) to determine which college or university a student may apply to
   (B) to give universities a standardized test with which to assess a student's academic aptitude
   (C) to measure what rank a potential student will likely graduate in his class
   (D) to assist companies to recruit future employees

3. Students can avoid taking the SAT by -------.
   (A) writing a letter to the president of the university
   (B) demonstrating that they get along well with fellow classmates
   (C) first taking a few classes part-time, and doing well in them
   (D) working part-time while attending school full-time

4. American students who do not maintain good grades are -------.
   (A) not usually able to graduate
   (B) not able to graduate unless they retake the SAT
   (C) not always required to take the GPA exam
   (D) not required to improve their academic scores

問 2. 次の定義が意味する語（句）を本文中から選びなさい。
1. a standard for making a decision (   )
2. a system which measures academic ability, based on grades (   )
3. a document containing student's courses and grades (   )
4. enough, proper (   )
5. to officially stop a student coming to school for a time (   )

Unit 15
CANADA

大自然を満喫できるカナダでは、アウトドア向けのブランド商品が多く作られています。最近は日本でもカナダブランドを見かけるようになりました。ここでは Louis Garneau という会社をとりあげます。

Listening Practice CD 30

次の出だし英文を読んでから、そのあとに流れる英文を聴き、1. ～ 3. の問いに適当な答えを (A) ～ (C) より選びなさい。

Canadian bicycle brand, Louis Garneau, was established in 1983.

1. Who is Louis Garneau?
   (A)   (B)   (C)

2. What makes the brand popular these days?
   (A)   (B)   (C)

3. Why do Louis Garneau bicycles attract fans from all over the world?
   (A)   (B)   (C)

Vocabulary, Grammar & Reading Comprehension

次の会話文を読んで下の問いに答えなさい。

日本の大学で社会学を専攻している Rieko はカナダのボランティアについて関心があります。そこでカナダから日本の大学に留学中の Jean に質問しています。

Rieko: Hi Jean! I just heard that you are (A) to do volunteer work next summer during your vacation.

Jean: That's right. I was thinking about getting a part-time job to (B) money. But ᴬ[better / thought / it / be / I / volunteer / to / would].

Rieko: Why? You can't make money doing volunteer work. You have to pay for your tuition and rent.

Jean: True, but I have a little money, and I have to think about my future, too. Volunteering is good job training, and (C) experience can be gained.

Rieko: I understand. How do you find a volunteer job? What kind of work are you looking for?

Jean: ᴮ[work / is / to / volunteer / it / easy / find]. You just have to go to the community center or to the university student center and find out what's (D). I'm hoping to (E) for work in childhood education at the YMCA, or at a summer camp, because I plan to be an elementary school teacher.

---

tuition 授業料　**YMCA** Young Man's Christian Association: キリスト教青年会。キリスト教主義に立ち、教育・スポーツ・福祉・文化などの分野の事業を展開する非営利公益団体。　**summer camp** 長期休暇の間に小中学生等を対象として行われるキャンプ。活動内容はハイキング、カヌーなどアウトドア系のものが多いが、最近は、演劇、ロック音楽、コンピュータの講習などを盛り込んだものもある。

問 1. 文中の (A) から (E) に入れるのに最も適当なものを下からそれぞれ選びなさい。

　　　　available　　apply　　earn　　planning　　valuable

問 2. 文中の A、B の [ ] 内の語を正しい順番に並べ替えて意味が通るようにしなさい。

A _____

B _____

問 3. 下の 1.～3. の英文が会話の内容に合っていれば T、間違っていれば F を選びなさい。

1. T F　Jean can pay for tuition with money earned from volunteering.
2. T F　Volunteering in Canada can provide students with valuable experience.
3. T F　Rieko understands why Canadian students willingly apply for volunteer work.

TOEIC Reading Practice & Vocabulary

次の英文を読んで下の問に答えなさい。

English and French are the official languages of Canada. In the Canadian census of 2011, it was reported that 98 percent of people were able to conduct a conversation either in English or in French, while only 17.5 percent can speak both English and French. Most of the French speakers live in Eastern Canada in places like Quebec.

According to the Vancouver City School Board, the demand for French Immersion programs has been increasing in Vancouver since 2006. One reason for the increase in demand is because parents who had French Immersion education, are seeking French Immersion schools for their children. Parents choose French Immersion for a variety of reasons. Some believe that speaking another language improves memory and brain development, while others hope it will lead to successful employment. Canadian parents report that Canadians who are bilingual in English and French have lower unemployment rates and a better chance of finding employment, and that their average incomes are 10 percent higher.

There are currently 14 elementary schools in Vancouver that offer French Immersion. Parents apply yearly for their children's enrollment, but students are currently chosen by lottery, because of high demand.

Vancouver　カナダ南西部の太平洋に面した港湾都市　　school board　教育委員会　　immersion program　外国語を身につける学習方法の一つ。目標とする言語を使いながら他の教科を学び、その過程で自然に言語を学ぶ手法。1960年代にカナダで始まった。　　bilingual　二か国語を話す

Unit 15

問 1. 本文の内容に合うように、(A)〜(D) の中から最も適当なものを選びなさい。

1. The Majority of people in Canada are able to speak, -------.
    (A) both English and French
    (B) either English or French
    (C) neither English or French
    (D) only English

2. Vancouver City School Board says -------.
    (A) that demand for French Immersion programs has increased
    (B) that demand for French Immersion programs has decreased
    (C) that demand for French Immersion programs is lower than it was previously
    (D) that demand for French Immersion programs has dramatically decreased

3. Parents choose French Immersion for their children because -------.
    (A) they hope French Immersion education will lead to lower employment opportunities
    (B) they hope French Immersion education will lead to business opportunities in Vancouver
    (C) they believe that French Immersion education helps children to make friends
    (D) they believe that French Immersion education helps memory and brain development

4. Because of the high demand for French Immersion programs, -------.
    (A) students will be enrolled by dropping by the school
    (B) students will be enrolled by lottery
    (C) students will be enrolled by passing an entrance examination
    (D) students will be enrolled according to their competence in French

問 2. 次の定義が意味する語（句）を本文中から選びなさい。

1. an official process or survey of counting a country's population (   )
2. to be placed into something   (   )
3. someone who speaks two languages   (   )
4. not having a job   (   )
5. a system used to decide who will get or be given   (   )
   something by a random drawing

編集者・執筆者一覧

編著者

山下 巖　　西村厚子　　デレック・イーベル　　淺間正通

著者

佐野哲子　　須部宗生　　田中裕実　　田村敏広　　中村善雄

編集協力

増田玲子

著作権法上、無断複写・複製は禁じられています。

Global Business Trends　　　　　　　　　　　　　　　　　[B-789]
英語でみる世界の大学生の就職事情

1 刷	2015年 2月 23日
3 刷	2021年10月 26日

編著者	山下　巖	Iwao Yamashita
	西村　厚子	Atsuko Nishimura
	デレック・イーベル	Derek Eberl
	淺間　正通	Masamichi Asama

発行者	南雲　一範　Kazunori Nagumo
発行所	株式会社　南雲堂
	〒162-0801　東京都新宿区山吹町361
	NAN'UN-DO Co., Ltd.
	361 Yamabuki-cho, Shinjuku-ku, Tokyo 162-0801, Japan
	振替口座：00160-0-46863
	TEL: 03-3268-2311(代表)／FAX: 03-3269-2486
	編集者　加藤　敦

製版	橋本　佳子
装丁	Nスタジオ
検印	省略
コード	ISBN 978-4-523-17789-0　C0082

Printed in Japan

E-mail　nanundo@post.email.ne.jp
URL　https://www.nanun-do.co.jp/

南雲堂のTOEIC対策本！

**トントン拍子でスコア・アップ！
夢をかなえる学習法！**

ネコの『トントン』

英語の師匠 オーガ＆セイン プレゼンツ
TOEIC® テスト攻略 トントンメソッド

- 特長1 **コロコロ**覚えるTOEIC頻出英単語！
- 特長2 **ドンドン**読めるスピード・リーディング！
- 特長3 **グングン**わかるシャドーイング！

デイビッド・セイン

大賀リヱ

◎ 銅メダルコース <Book 1>
　　TOEIC 400点～600点レベル（154ページ）

◎ 銅メダルコース <Book 2>
　　TOEIC 500点～700点レベル（154ページ）

◎ 銀メダルコース
　　TOEIC 600点～800点レベル（160ページ）

◎ 金メダルコース
　　TOEIC 700点～（180ページ）

大賀リヱ・デイビッド・セイン著／46判　定価（各本体1000円＋税）

南雲堂の英語書

**リスニング＋リーディングに頻出
音で聞いて、目で見て、
ズバリ対応！**

本書の特徴

- 精選された TOEIC® テスト頻出単語とイディオム
- レベル別とテーマ別に分類
- 必須単語を例文の中で確認し、覚えることができる
- 赤チェックシート学習
- 文法の弱点補強ができる
- CD 音声でリスニングの訓練ができる

新 TOEIC® テストズバリ出る英単語ファイル
赤チェックシート付

三原　京著

A5 判　295 ページ CD2 枚付　定価 (本体 2,000 円＋税)
ISBN978-4-523-26482-8

南雲堂
NAN'UN-DO

南雲堂
英語語学書最新刊!!

やっぱり、やっぱり英文法!!
英文法をやさしく学ぶ1ヵ月イメージトレーニングメソッド

イラスト＋写真で
1ヵ月スピードマスター **英文法『イメトレ』**

アンドルー・ベネット 著
小宮 徹

A5判（166ページ）
定価（本体1,400円＋税）
7月中旬刊行予定

MP3 CD付

比較
The car is **faster than** the motorcycle.

副詞節
She talks on the phone **before she rides her bike.**

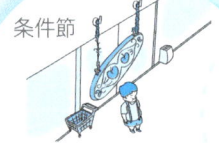

be動詞
She **is** surprised.

条件節
If the sign **falls**, the boy **may be** hurt.

未来
The race **will be** very close.

副詞
The dog is **extremely** large.

「言葉」ではなく「イメージ」で学ぶ英文法
これ1冊で中学〜高校で学習する英文法を完全理解
日本人学習者のやり直し英語にも最適

南雲堂
〒162-0801
東京都新宿区山吹町361
TEL 03-3268-2384　FAX 03-3260-5425